Out OF EGYPT

Out of Egypt

A JOURNEY OUT OF BONDAGE AND OPPRESSION

TONYA R. MCCLURE

OUT OF EGYPT:
A JOURNEY OUT OF BONDAGE AND OPPRESSION

Copyright © 2016 by Tonya R. McClure

All rights reserved. No part of this publication may be reproduced, distributed, or transmitted in any form or by any means, including photocopying, recording, or other electronic or mechanical methods, without the prior written permission of the publisher, except in the case of brief quotations embodied in critical reviews and certain other noncommercial uses permitted by copyright law.

All scripture quotations, unless otherwise indicated are taken from the King James Bible version.

ISBN 978-1-945456-18-3

Printed in the United States of America

Cover Design: Warrior Design

Editor: Danese Frazier Turner

DEDICATIONS

To all people who have overcome every obstacle that has attempted to hinder and abort their God-ordained destiny.

This book is dedicated to Teia Hopewell, a fellow graduate of Eagle's International Training Institute and in memory of the late Soror Anedra S. Williams.

TABLE OF CONTENTS

Acknowledgements

Foreword

Introduction

Chapter 1: **The Beginning**	1
Chapter 2: **Wilderness**	15
Chapter 3: **Journey**	25
Chapter 4: **Exodus**	37
Chapter 5: **Shift**	49
Chapter 6: **A New Day**	61
Conclusion	71

ACKNOWLEDGMENTS

Thank you to the following individuals who without their contributions and support this book would not have been written:

Pastor Wilbur T. Purvis
Pastor Rekesha Pittman
Apostle Kevin Nelson
Minister Stacy Lloyd
Minister Danese Turner
Minister Kelley I. Brown
Minister Traci L. Draper

FOREWORD

Someone has appropriately proclaimed that, "Life is a journey not a destination." On the heels of that proclamation and further validating its truth, Minister Tonya McClure, releases her debut book entitled, "Out of Egypt." This book is not a specialized treaty for the lazy, nor a handbook for individuals stuck in mediocrity but a road map for aspiring believers from all walks of life making their journey from life's narrow confines of bondage to the liberating scenic views of freedom.

Tonya allows the reader to take a front seat view and witness first-hand how God strategically guides the footsteps of our lives by constantly shifting and stretching us toward growth and maturity. The beauty of riding in the front seat of her life is we are privy to see how she crosses over speed bumps, deals with detours, manages GPS mis-calibrations and ultimately arrives safely at God's intended destination on time and in sync with God's plan.

The children of Israel wandered aimlessly for 40 years because of their own disobedience, insecurity and doubt. The wilderness which was intended to be a temporary pit stop became their permanent parking space until God raised a new generation of willing and obedient travelers whose sights were set on the Promised Land. You are a part of that new generation whose destiny is the Promised Land. This book will be a confirmation that the gates have been opened and access has been granted.

All the traffic signs of this inspiring book, "Out of Egypt," point to the scriptural wake-up call that God gave Israel in Deuteronomy 2:3, "You have circled this mountain long enough. Now turn north." I believe it is no coincidence that this book has landed into your hands—no matter where you find yourself in this meandering journey called life. Whether you are reading this book on your train ride to work or laying across the bed in your dormitory room or vacationing on the sun-kissed beaches of the Caribbean Islands, God wants to remind you that He never intended for you live a perpetual life of bondage nor oppression. Pack your bags! Turn north! You are headed, "Out of Egypt."

Your fellow traveler,

Wilbur T. Purvis III
Lead Pastor
Destiny World Church

INTRODUCTION

Merriam Webster Collegiate Dictionary defines a journey as "an act of traveling from one place to another." It also defines the word exodus as "a situation in which many people leave a place at the same time." Many of us, believers and non-believers are familiar with the Book of Exodus in the Bible and the illustration of the Israelites' journey through the wilderness for 40 years and finally the deliverance out of Egypt and from the hand of Pharaoh. I am inviting you to accompany me on this journey and explore how we often get stranded in foreign places for indefinite periods of time, with no road map or strategies for an expeditious exit.

When we study the significance of the number 40, it becomes clear that this number is of monumental importance because it represents a period of testing or judgment. This is significant because it also represents the length of time necessary to accomplish some major part of God's plan in His dealings with His people. The number 40 can also represent gestation, resting and resurrection. This is important to understand because many of us can spend minutes, hours, days, months or years in places where time moves forward and we remain stagnant, non-progressive, not in a posture or position of birthing because we allowed ourselves to be bound by our circumstances, situations, challenges, road blocks, detours, miscalibrated GPS system and just completely lost.

When I think back over my entire life, I now realize that every obstacle, disappointment, derailment, denial and distraction was a set-up to build my character. I can acknowledge God's hand, provision and protection along the way. I have learned to be strong in the midst of the storm, patient, persistent and prepared to do all that God called me to do. God has blessed me immensely. God chose me because He equipped me to handle it. God loves me and keeps me. His promises are yes and Amen. This book focuses on how we can get delivered from the dry, dead places in our lives that keep us from pursuing our destiny, losing faith and staying encouraged.

CHAPTER 1

THE BEGINNING

The beginning is where our personal stories start. Our entire life is centered and structured around all that happened in the beginning. The beginning creates experiences, whether positive or negative, nevertheless an experience. *Webster's Dictionary* defines experience as "the process of doing and seeing things and of having things happen to you; skill or knowledge that you get by doing something; the length of time that you have spent doing something.

Growing up as a child I was very inquisitive and often needed to have mental stimulation to keep me occupied. I mastered many activities with ease and would frequently get bored when not challenged. This resulted in my often getting in trouble for misbehaving. (I now know that I was curious, not "bad", but my parents' generation was not educated on how best to deal with a personality type like mine). We grew up attending my grandmother's A.M.E. church as children, but were periodically allowed to worship at my parent's Baptist church on the 4th Sunday of each month. Now while I was too young to understand the significance of the differences of denominations as a child, I did realize that I seemed to have more "fun" when I went to my parent's church, but thank God for revelation. The wife of the pastor at my grandmother's church convinced my parents to allow my middle sister and me to take dance classes. Some ladies commented to my grandmother that "she does not know how to sit still in church; she needs to take dance to burn some of that energy." The seed was planted! I started dancing at the age of 6 and haven't stopped since. I also was more academically advanced than most students my age and skipped a grade in elementary school which caused me to always be the youngest in my class by age, but always less mature. Both my sister and I went to school out of district and because my parents had only one vehicle, we took public transportation to and from school unescorted at a very young age. Those were the days.

My father served in the Navy; worked as a plasterer and enjoyed playing golf immensely on one of the few courses in Atlanta that allowed African American to play. He was a proud member of The Golfer's Twelve. My mother worked in child care, drove the transportation van and cooked at a Jewish Montessori school. Both my sister and I were fortunate to have attended the school and have the experience of Jewish culture and the diversity of exploring other cultures at a young age. It was during a summer camp at the Jewish Montessori School that I had a traumatic swimming incident but that's another story. My grandmother lived with us and stayed home. She prepared hot breakfast every

THE BEGINNING

morning before school and dinner was prepared upon our return from school, what a blessing. As a child, I recall looking forward to going "downtown" on Saturday mornings to shop with my grandmother.

Again this experience taught me at an early age how to navigate public transportation, read street signs and understand directions. What I did not realize at that time was the life lessons my grandmother was implanting in my memory. She was a praying woman and each morning she was up at 5AM reading scripture, praying and singing gospel music (the AM station that was playing on the radio). She also insisted that everyone in the house attend church on Sunday no matter what. Grandma would prepare Sunday dinner on Saturday evening so after church all she needed to do was warm it up. I also vividly recall Saturday night television time including watching *The Lawrence Welk show, Hee Haw and World Wide Wrestling* (yes we were exposed).

In 1979, my mother passed away unexpectedly and my world changed forever. I am certain that this took a toll on my grandmother, given that my mother was her youngest child. A few years later, Grandma suffered a major stroke which rendered her needing fulltime care and being placed in a nursing home. My oldest sister moved in to care for my sister and I while we finished middle and high school. My father eventually remarried. And then the ultimate blow. During my senior year of high school, I got pregnant and had a son. This was a life-altering experience but one that became the catalyst for defining my character today.

Many people, especially the elder members of my grandmother's church wrote me off, spoke negatively about me, most likely saying "I wouldn't amount anything." Obviously my family was extremely disappointed. But while my school endeavors and dance career was delayed, it was not derailed.

My son was born during the Thanksgiving break; I only missed two weeks of school and returned to classes in January with all of the other students. I became even more determined to prove to the naysayers that I could finish high school, go to college and become successful. I was deeply hurt by the negative comments and piercing looks that members of the church gave me. I just could not understand how people could be so mean and nasty and lack compassion. Nevertheless, I finished in the top 10% of my high school class, was recognized by my classmates as the "Most Talented," "Most Popular" and "Most Congenial" student and was honored to dance at my high school graduation.

I enrolled in college in August of that year at a liberal arts school that was several miles from my home. I didn't have a car, so I once again had to take public transportation to get to an 8:00 am class. The college was a predominantly white institution and this was the first time since Montessori school that I personally had attended classes with non-minorities.

My freshman year was a challenge trying to balance being a mother and a student. I did well in some subjects and not so well in others, but I was determined not to fail school because that is what everyone expected me to do. I had a part-time job on

THE BEGINNING

campus for a while and by my junior year, I was working full time and going to school part time. I bought my first car and no longer had to take the BUS! I finished college in five years and obtained my Bachelor's degree in Human Resources Administration.

Because of my many years of work, I was able to transition to a better position on my career path with the company I was working for. During these years, I realized just how supportive both my family and my son's father's family were by encouraging me to finish school.

Shortly after my college graduation, my son started elementary school and became very active in baseball, football, basketball and Cub Scouts. I also became engaged during that time and was planning a wedding when the relationship became abusive. With my son in tow, I abruptly left the man and residence. While I was determined not to have to go back home, I did stay with my sister temporarily while the domestic violence case moved through the judicial system and ran its course so that I could move back in to the home I shared with my then fiancé. The relationship did ultimately end, but that was just another life experience that tested my resiliency to overcome the odds.

When my son started middle school, I started graduate school. I now understand how critical it was to have the unwavering love and support of family and extended family. I also understand that the level of love, sacrifice and support that I received played a major role in my becoming the woman that I am. Oh yeah, I might add that at some point in all of this I stopped attending church (although I knew my grandmother would not approve) because of the hurtful treatment I received during my pregnancy. Nonetheless, I continued to prove the doubters wrong.

I completed graduate school; purchased my current home and my son started high school. I did start attending church again and got reconnected in a way that made me feel welcomed and appreciated. In addition, the practical teaching helped coach and develop me more. A few years later, my father passed of renal failure. My son was leaving to go to college and yet another relationship failed.

I went in to a state of depression. It was a dark, deep place I had never been before. It seemed that I had lost everything.

I remember going to church that Sunday (obviously looking beat up and worn out) and one of the evangelists looked at me and said "Just let it go. It's going to be alright." My first thought was, "How did she know?" However, I have grown and matured in the Word of God and now better understand the spirit of discernment. Her statement really was the confirmation I needed to get my raggedy self together and move on with life.

Today, this evangelist is one of my best mentors and still speaks life into every area of my life. She has gotten connected with my immediate family and loves, guides and supports us spiritually in so many ways. I became more involved in church (including the dance ministry, single's ministry, church school, new member's orientation and Bible study). My previous dance ministry leader would frequently speak over me that I was destined to teach and pastor. I fought that prophetic word for a number of years, not even knowing it was prophetic at the time, because of my fears of being inadequate, not well-versed in the Word, questioning why God would want to use me. After all, I'm a sinner.

For many years I battled self-esteem issues and struggled with trusting myself (God is still working on that spirit in me). I did not realize how much self-trust and confidence affected and impacted every area of my life. I enjoyed studying and completing Eagles International Training Institute (EITI), leadership training and every opportunity I had to attend conferences or workshops to teach me more about God and who I am in Him.

In 2009, I was offered the opportunity to join the ministerial alliance team at my church. I agreed on the condition that I would not have to preach. REALLY! Or so I thought... For more than a year, I studied, trained, and completed assignments and fellowshipped with the "more seasoned" ministers to learn various aspects and responsibilities of church leadership and ministry. I made contributions to ministry by teaching classes based on life lessons I had learned along the way.

While I faithfully danced before the congregation on a regular basis, I had absolutely no desire to speak in front of them. I frequently taught movement, leadership and biblical foundations for dancers all across the United States, but still had a fear of speaking before my church body. Then it finally happened. I received a call from our ministry Elder requesting that I preach. I must have cried for three days straight. Even though I thought of every reason why the Elder should pick someone else, I wrote out my message, had five different people critique it and still felt inadequate to go before God's people and deliver a sermon.

The morning of the sermon message, I cried for 40 minutes before I went in to the sanctuary. I felt troubled that I was not prepared enough and would embarrass myself. For many years Proverbs 3:5-6 *Trust in the LORD with all your heart and lean not on your own understanding; in all your ways submit to him, and he will make your paths straight*" had become my "go to" scripture. But I failed to realize that Proverbs 3:5-6 was manifesting itself through me at that very moment. My "aha" moment came when I realized that everything and I do mean *everything* in my life had prepared me for that moment. The sermon title was "When you can't see your ditches" and the sermon theme focused on when things are before you that you can't really see, God already has a plan to detour you around them. While the detour may take you on a longer route, you can reach your destination; you just see it from a different perspective.

Merriam Webster defines perception as "a way of regarding, understanding, or interpreting something; mental impression; Perspective is a particular attitude toward or way of regarding something; a point a view." All of our experiences in life frame our mindset, build our belief system and influence our perceptions.

These experiences then provide our perspective for every future endeavor.

> **Isaiah 43:19**
>
> *"Behold, I will do a new thing; now it shall spring forth; shall ye not know it? I will even make a way in the wilderness, and rivers in the desert."*

THOUGHTS ON MY WAY OUT OF EGYPT:

MY BEGINNING

THOUGHTS ON MY WAY OUT OF EGYPT:

MY BEGINNING

_____

_____

_____

_____

_____

_____

_____

_____

_____

_____

_____

CHAPTER 2

WILDERNESS

The wilderness is defined as:

> A tract or region uncultivated and uninhabited by human beings; an area essentially undisturbed by human activity together with its naturally developed life community; an empty or pathless area or region; a part of a garden devoted to wild growth; obsolete: wild or uncultivated state; a confusing multitude or mass: an indefinitely great number or quantity; a bewildering situation.

A popular Bible story gives us a vivid illustration of how God sometimes works in strange ways. Perhaps you are familiar with the exodus of the Israelites from Pharaoh, but even beyond that story, we still see the mysteries of God and His grace and mercy even after the birth of The Messiah. This would suggest that wilderness experiences can reach and impact anyone.

Our experiences might not be completely comprehensible most of the time, but there is a purpose for each encounter and a lesson to be learned from them all. After Jesus was baptized, the next thing He experienced was temptation. Even Jesus Christ is led into the wilderness by the Holy Spirit, where he is tempted by Satan, His adversary. Likewise is the nature of our own wilderness experiences where we often question why we were brought to certain places or down certain paths.

As with the Jews, the wilderness can evoke many emotions and memories. Most familiar is their 40-year journey out of Egypt. What we must come to accept is that the wilderness is a place of vulnerability, a difficult experience in an unfamiliar place with uncertain provisions (Exodus 15:22-24; 16:2-3). In that story, the wilderness was a place of testing where the promises of God were all they had (Deuteronomy 8:1-5).The wilderness was not just a place of vulnerability for the Jews. It was also a place of transition that lay between their slavery and liberation (Exodus 3:17). Jesus' wilderness experience marked a transition for Him too. Sometimes we must recognize that the wilderness experience is a point of preparation for the place where we are being elevated and exposed.

Oppression

Have you ever had a wilderness experience? Was it a time of vulnerability, brokenness and testing far away from all that is comfortable, familiar and promised? It usually involves a risky step of faith, a season of doubt, or it can be a point of rebellion and disobedience. However during the time of preparation God was preparing you for meaningful and powerful work.

The wilderness can be a dark, frightful, lonely place that causes you anxiety and fear because of the multitude of unknown dangers. We must continue to recognize who God was to Israel and who He is to us individually. As you remember Jesus Christ, our deliverer, you might realize that your wilderness experience may actually prove to be your transition into an unprecedented period of fruitfulness.

How do we get oppressed in our mindset, thoughts and actions? While there are a number of definitions of the word oppressed, the one that struck a chord with me was "the state of being subject to unjust treatment or control." Oppressed is synonymous with persecution, abuse, maltreatment, suppression, subjection; cruelty, brutality, injustice, hardship, suffering, misery; mental pressure or distress.

When I think about the number of disloyal friendships, bad and unhealthy relationships, missed promotional opportunities at work, loss of loved ones and the countless times my efforts and achievements have been overlooked or gone unrecognized by someone or someone else takes credit for the work that I do, it seemed easy for me to get to a place of oppression and have a difficult time moving on. I even took the position, "Why should I do anymore? It's not worth it." But God showed me differently. I am worth it to Him and to the Kingdom.

This period of transition and transformation was pivotal in teaching me and revealing to me that God is faithful when we genuinely and authentically serve Him. God does not let disappointment and hurt keep us down for too long.

During the wilderness experience of the Israelites, there were periods where they got hungry, other times when they got thirsty. At times like this, instead of remembering God's great and mighty works from the past, and trusting Him, the Israelites frequently complained against Moses and against God. At other times they spoke of going back to Egypt. They remembered the food they enjoyed there, and seemed to have forgotten what it was like to be a slave under cruel taskmasters. They just wanted to go back to Egypt.

Bondage

The Israelites' attitude mirrored the attitude and behaviors of Christians who, after a difficult season in the wilderness, despise God and His promises and want to return to the world and its pleasures. We often make excuses and justify why it's okay to return to an unhealthy and unfulfilling relationship. Even when we know that someone does not respect us or have an admiration for our great qualities, we still entertain that person under the guise of "love for all of God's people." Stop it!

God wants us to love ourselves **first** before we love anyone else more than we love ourselves or God himself. But we fail to recognize this as a form of oppression. We justify remaining in unfulfilling assignments in church and ministry by saying "I am serving the Lord." He never intended for us to serve Him passively, but to fulfill our destinies through His teachings and the manifestation of His glory being revealed through us.

How can you get to that place when you consciously choose to remain in situations that don't breathe any life into your lungs and help you grow and develop in to that being that God has designed you to be? Stop making excuses and start making progress. Slaves in America did not go free because their minds had been conditioned that if they left the plantation, they would be killed. Don't die in a place that God never intended for you to die.

We should never allow experiences to put us in bondage without a way of escape. 1 Corinthians 10:13 instructs us "There hath no temptation taken you but such as is common to man: but God is faithful, who will not suffer you to be tempted above that ye are able; but will with the temptation also make a way to escape, that ye may be able to bear it." God is faithful.

Mature Christians never deny God's faithfulness. We have all sinned, been tempted and questioned if God would keep His word and be faithful to us. There is no mistake in God's unadulterated word: "If we are faithless He remains faithful, for He cannot deny Himself" (2 Timothy 2:13). God's faithfulness always overcomes. God promised His faithfulness to Israel, God was faithful to David after he sinned with Bathsheba. God was faithful to Peter after he denied

Jesus three times. God was faithful to Daniel in the lion's den and Shadrach, Meshach, and Abednego in the fiery furnace.

Why would God not keep His promise to you and take you through your wilderness experience? Through my journey in the wilderness I had to recognize His hand in every situation and understand His protection. Some of the dysfunction, disruptive and disturbing experiences I encountered were really the canvas for building my character. I learned a lot from those experiences and so will you.

Ephesians 5:20

"Giving thanks always for all things unto God and the Father in the name of our Lord Jesus Christ"

THOUGHTS ON MY WAY OUT OF EGYPT:

MY WILDERNESS STORY

_____

_____

_____

_____

_____

_____

_____

_____

_____

_____

_____

THOUGHTS ON MY WAY OUT OF EGYPT:

MY WILDERNESS STORY

_____

_____

_____

_____

_____

_____

_____

_____

_____

_____

CHAPTER 3

JOURNEY

A journey is an act of traveling from one place to another. Think about your journey, think about your "wilderness experience" when it comes to facing temptation and times of testing. When have you been led down paths of destruction or dead ends with seemingly no way out? Have you ever found yourself stuck in a ditch and not sure how you would get out or had to successfully navigate through the wilderness? If so, what was the key to your survival?

The book of Jeremiah teaches primarily the message of judgment on Judah for their rampant idolatry. But later in the text, God promises restoration of Judah back to the land God had given them.

The prophet Jeremiah is known as a faithful servant who courageously and faithfully declared God's word despite at times being alone in declaring his message. Jeremiah's early messages were a call to repentance for condemnation of Judah for their false worship and social injustices. Jeremiah's prophecies had been critical of the people's dependence on the temple as a place of security and their selfishness and materialism, much like many of us who rely on the security of tangible things as a source of our comfort and protection. Jeremiah often preached messages of doom and the messages were full of bad news. Jeremiah was not a popular messenger, but he was prophetic. Jeremiah had his prophetic writings burned, was thrown into prison and then later tossed into a cistern. Jeremiah also suffered from internal doubt and conflict about what he had been called to do.

Now how many of us have days like Jeremiah's when everything someone says or does is negative? How many times have we questioned ourselves, when God directed us to do something or even questioned that it was really God? The thing we can learn from Jeremiah's character was Jeremiah believed in his messages and he had a determined resolve and passion to compel people to change their ways.

When he started on his journey, Jeremiah probably did not expect to encounter the roadblocks, distractions, obstacles and challenges he did, but Jeremiah remained obedient to his call. God ultimately rewarded Jeremiah because of his obedience despite what others had to say. Jeremiah realized that his assignment was bigger than who he was, how other people perceived him and Jeremiah fully operated in his prophetic calling. He was special and knew his gift was special, therefore, he ascribed to being more than just average or mediocre.

Many times we are faced with difficult situations in life. We feel lonely, as if we are the only ones experiencing this challenge. We ask the question, "Why did this happen to me?" The path we are on may seem dark and dismal as if there is no way out. But ditches and potholes show up unexpectedly, and when they do, they grab our attention. There are times when God is intentionally trying to grab our attention to enable us to take some action.

Unfortunate events happen. This does not always mean we have been cursed, that the devil is attacking us or God is not with us. Much like Jeremiah, we must stay committed to our purpose and relentlessly pursue what God has called us to be despite hindrances that may seemingly get in our way.

Often times, things do not appear as we see them in the natural. Sometimes we can speak judgment over our lives by the thoughts in our minds and the words spoken from our mouths. Many of us know our family well, our jobs, our favorite sports team, our favorite restaurant and so on and so forth. But as soon as difficulties come our way, we forget that we know the God of all creation, Maker of heaven and earth, Ruler of all things, the Alpha and Omega, the Beginning and the End.

In May 2011, I was attending a local high school graduation. The school had very limited parking for the more than 1000 people attending the graduation ceremony. I arrived late and had to park across the street at the elementary school. The only parking area available was on a grassy lot where we had to navigate the curb to reach the parking. At that time, there was still some daylight left.

I attended the ceremony and had the epiphany that "If I leave a little early, I can get ahead of the traffic." When I originally arrived to park, there were individuals directing traffic and parking. When I returned to my vehicle, the individuals directing the parking were gone. So I was on my own to get out of the grassy lot and leave before the traffic jam ensued.

When I got in the car, there appeared to be an open area where I could just drive a short distance and get back on the main road without having to go back over that curb. I thought, "Perfect, I can get out of here quickly and easily." However, little did I know that the bump of the curve was divinely orchestrated to be a safer exit than my impending attempt to exit quickly. That bump was there to remind me that in every situation, I need to acknowledge that God's plan is to protect me, to protect me from hurt, harm and danger, seen and unseen.

As I proceeded to exit, my car dropped off a bit and I wondered, "Hum, what's that?" Well, as fate would have it, it was now dark outside. I then opened my car door and immediately realized I had just run in to the edge of a culvert. I got back in the car and attempted to back out, but because of rain earlier in the day, I could not get any traction to get my front wheel out. I immediately began to panic and thought my car was going to plunge forward and crash with me in it. There were a few people leaving (mostly women) and I yelled, "Please find a police officer! Call 911!" By then I was really nervous.

The graduation ceremony concluded and people were beginning to exit. There was a family coming by who saw my situation. The three men in the group offered to help try to push the car out of the culvert and asked me to steer the car. I was way too shaken up to try to move the car again and asked one of them to drive. At that moment, as more people were leaving and four young men were coming across the street, I began to question why I panicked and was nervous about this situation. God had already kept His promise as written in Hebrews 13:5: "I will never leave you nor forsake you (NIV)." I was also arrested in my spirit of 2 Timothy 1:7 "For God hath not given us the spirit of fear; but of power, and of love, and of a sound mind." In that moment I had to put my mind on God and allow the angelic help of the Lord to do the rest. First of all, it was just a car. Secondly, God had given me the wisdom to get out of the car, and thirdly, if it crashed in to the culvert, God had already given me the protection I needed: my insurance coverage was paid.

There was a plan. No matter what the outcome of the vehicle, God was protecting me all the time. I just needed to declare to myself that God's word said that His plan was to prosper me and not to harm me. I also had to remind myself that in this situation as is written in Proverbs 3:5-6 to "Trust in the Lord with all thine heart and lean not to thine own understanding. In all thy ways acknowledge him and he shall direct your path." When I began to realize

God's real plan for me, I had to know that it was Him that I needed to trust to deal with that situation.

Once you begin to know that you know, you will begin to realize that in the midst of your worse situations—loss of a job, loss of a loved one, depression, sickness, financial difficulties, loneliness—don't forget that God does have a plan.

The situations and circumstances that come up in our lives are indeed a setup. Sometimes God needs to get our attention quickly. Sometimes He will let things happen in a subtle way and sometimes it is not so subtle.

We know multiple characters from the Bible who were faced with what can be perceived as an obstacle, but they successfully and creatively shifted from the obstacle to an opportunity. Moses had an obstacle (born a Hebrew but leads the Israelites out of Egypt towards the Promised Land). Joseph had some obstacles (sold, accused, imprisoned but he never lost faith and saved a nation from starvation). Esther had an obstacle (she had to hide her Jewish descent from her husband, but eventually she saved her people). David had some obstacles (Bathsheba and Goliath). Daniel had an obstacle (lion's den). Shadrach, Meshach, Abednego had an obstacle (a fiery furnace). Paul had some obstacles (he initially persecuted the church as Saul and was temporarily blinded, but he went on to become one of the greatest evangelists). But what we see in all these individuals is that out of all of their obstacles, they created opportunities and achieved greatness. They did not allow what others may have perceived as an obstacle to hinder them from pursuing their destinies.

All of them realized that to mentally defeat their obstacle became their greatest opportunity. It is only when you lose or miss the opportunity; that it becomes an obstacle to you. When you "know that you know," things don't always seem to be as they appear. God's word says He plans to give you hope. Hope means "the feeling that what is wanted can be had or that events will turn out for the best."

Don't avoid your obstacles because you see them as destructive; begin to believe that which you can't see. Hebrews 11:1 says, "Now faith is the substance of things hoped for, the evidence of things not seen." We know that there is plan, and because of the plan, God makes provision according to Philippians 4:19.

Stop standing around, worrying about all the things that appear to be wrong right now. God created us in His image and since He created us in His image, everything we say and do should reflect His image.

God never worried, doubted, gave up hope or threw in the white towel. God wants you to know that He is in control and He has already worked it out for your good. Be confident in this: God is getting ready to prosper you.

He purposed you for such a time as this so that he could activate His plan, reveal His protection, and progress you towards your future. You "know that you know" gives you the capacity to see what you can't see right now, because your faith causes you to believe that no matter what comes your way, with God by your side, every obstacle becomes an opportunity for you to know YES I CAN.

Trust in God in the midst of knowing and not knowing. Proclaim your job, proclaim your healing, proclaim reconciliation, proclaim abundance and overflow in your finances. Proclaim "I am more than a conqueror and I am victorious!"

> **John 10:10**
>
> *"The thief cometh not, but for to steal, and to kill, and to destroy: I am come that they might have life, and that they might have it more abundantly."*

THOUGHTS ON MY WAY OUT OF EGYPT:

MY MEMORABLE JOURNEY

_____

_____

_____

_____

_____

_____

_____

_____

_____

_____

THOUGHTS ON MY WAY OUT OF EGYPT:

MY MEMORABLE JOURNEY

_____

_____

_____

_____

_____

_____

_____

_____

_____

_____

_____

_____

CHAPTER 4

EXODUS

An exodus is defined as "the act or an instance of going out." This suggests that we must be purposeful and intentional to get out of some places that were never intended for us. Many of us are guilty of taking up residence or squatting in dry and dead places that are not healthy, meaningful, and purposeful for our growth and development and for reaching our destinies.

Life experiences and scriptures have revealed to us that after a period of joy and blessing we will eventually enter a dry wilderness. This is not to say that we will be dry spiritually. Depending upon how we allow life to happen and how we manage what happens, we could be dry mentally, physically, emotionally and spiritually.

God's will for us is to be filled with the Holy Spirit (Ephesians 5:18), and He does not withhold the Holy Spirit to those who obey Him. The Holy Spirit is the one who encourages us in good times and bad times. Let me be clear, even with the Holy Spirit, it is possible to go through a wilderness experience in which there is almost nothing in your circumstances to encourage you. There are times when you may just try to survive from day to day, emotionally, financially or materially. You are waiting for your healing to manifest. Your joy and peace have been violated by unfavorable emotions and thoughts, which you must gather the strength to resist. It is difficult, but remember God's promise that you will never be tempted beyond your ability to endure, and with each temptation He will also make a way of escape, that you may be able to bear it.

During this season of testing and trials, you will find the ordinary comforts of the world will not satisfy you. This is the time when you are forced to depend on God for all you need emotionally, physically and spiritually. Proverbs 3:5-6 reminds us to trust that the wilderness time is only temporary, and to diligently trust God for direction.

Jesus Christ went through a wilderness experience and He demonstrated how to navigate through it successfully. The same methods will work for any one of us. Christ lives in each of us to make this ability to navigate a possibility for us. The Lord is the strength of our life! (Isaiah 12:2; Psalm 27:1).

Anyone who has gotten anywhere in God has gone through at least one wilderness experience. It is normal to go through more than one dry or wilderness experience in your life. Wildernesses can be seasons to learn from God where there is no option. There is a waiting period between the time you receive a promise from God and the time of its fulfillment. God has not forgotten His promise to you and He hasn't given up on you. He is molding and shaping you through the wilderness experience to be the kind of person who can overcome giants through faith. Before you get there, you will be painfully tried and tested. Use each trial as an opportunity to be promoted to better things in God.

We know from the book of Exodus and Moses' and Jesus' own personal experiences that the length of time of a wilderness experience can vary from 40 days to 40 years. Your wilderness might only be a few days or many decades. Our efforts to maneuver God's dealings will determine how rapidly we get out and into the fruitfulness, forgiveness and fulfilled chapters of our lives. The Israelites could have been out of the wilderness in two years had they believed God's promises to them.

God does not forsake His principles for anyone. God does not play favorites, but responds to us according to what is in our hearts. The tests and trials are not required for God to know what is in our hearts, but rather for US to realize the genuineness of our hearts.

If we have a heart condition, it will be exposed when we are squeezed or under pressure. When God squeezes us and puts us under pressure, we find out whether our hearts are filthy and fake. This is why we should guard our hearts. What we permit, tolerate, engage in and allow to take root in our hearts determines what God will arrange for us to deal with in life. Proverbs 4:23 has already confirmed this: "Keep thy heart with all diligence; for out of it are the issues of life."

We've all heard the old cliché that patience is a virtue and faith and patience can get us out of the wilderness as quickly as possible. It is better to endure pain now than to go on suffering frustration for a lifetime until you learn the lesson and pass the test that God is putting before you now. At the same time, we must remember that there is power in speaking out God's Word according to Proverbs 18:21 "Death and life are in the power of the tongue: and they that love it shall eat the fruit thereof."

Speak God's word and proclaim in the name of Jesus, then release great spiritual power and authority to overcome the wiles of the enemy. Stand strong on His word and command with authority and the devil will be forced to flee because he recognizes that you are equipped and ready for battle. The foundation for all of your future blessings has already been established.

This is the time that your faith increases and grows and will demonstrate that you have the capacity to withstand the tests. God wants you to release to Him the opportunity to recover a return on His investment in you. God created us to worship Him in spirit and in truth. Your wilderness experience is a time to get to know God more intimately, and experience His grace and mercy in your life through your prayer and intercession. Trust that when your wilderness experience comes to an end, you will be on assignment fighting more giants than you ever imagined.

Because of your period of preparation and revelation, you will value the time you spent getting to know God more personally. Your foundation of discipline and training has provided you with the ability to escape backsliding as soon as God starts releasing blessing upon you. You will seek to use those resources for God. Your life will have immeasurable impact and you will shine like the stars in heaven for all eternity (Daniel 12:3). Don't give up in the midst of trials. It is necessary that you pass through seasons of trials, but God is there for you to strengthen you and hold you up.

"Run Forest Run"

We all remember the movie *Forest Gump* and the famous line "Run, Forest, Run!" At the beginning of the movie Forest Gump is running away from some bullies and the girl he likes, Jenny, is yelling to him "Run Forest Run!". How many times have we been in situations or encounters where we've clearly heard God say to us, for our own safety "Run, Forest, Run"? We knew it was not a good decision, was not beneficial, and was counterproductive to our progress. Nevertheless we refused to get out of the situation. Much like in the movie, we have been faced with some bullies but we failed to exercise the fortitude, wisdom, tenacity and courage to run.

Here are my F's for execution:

(a) **Flee** - "to run away from, to move swiftly." This is the decision-making step. What are you going to do, when are you going to do it; are you surrendering and giving up? Since flee is an action word, you have to decide what you are going to do and when you're going to do it. Some situations don't permit slothfulness or indecisiveness.

If a fire breaks out, how long does it take you to decide you are going to get out? If you had a heart attack and emergency responders waited to act or took their time to think about what measures to take to save your life, it would be the difference between life and death. The same applies to the matters we allow to consume our thoughts and minds and why we enable certain people, places and things to consume us and place a stronghold on us. When we refuse to act or act quickly, we refuse to set ourselves free from those dead, dry, brittle, broken, unharvestable situations.

(b) **Faith** - "confidence or trust in a person or thing; strong or unshakeable belief in something, esp. without proof or evidence." Hebrews 11:1 says, "Now faith is the substance of things hoped for, the evidence of things not seen." Most of us are real good at reciting this passage of scripture but we are terrible at *walking in* or manifesting this passage of scripture. Too often we want to see the results, the expectation met, the promised fulfilled, the proof that we were right. But what are we really waiting on? If faith is truly about the evidence of things *not* seen, then move by faith and trust that although you cannot visually see the manifestation, God already promised you in Jeremiah 29:11 "For I know the thoughts that I think toward you, saith the Lord, thoughts of peace, and not of evil, to give you an expected end."

(c) **Focus** (re-focus) - "a central point, as of attraction, attention, or activity; to direct one's attention or efforts." Since focus is about directing our efforts, when will we truly activate our energies for the purpose of reaching our destinies? Psalm 119:35 states it this way: "Make me to go in the path of thy commandments; for therein do I delight."

How can we expect to be and receive the delight of the Lord when we passively wait for something to happen or change? God never intended for us to remain stagnant in any area of our lives. He commanded us to fulfill each day by the assurances of His Word and promises, and that requires activation not complacency. Yes, this does mean you sometimes will need to change your address, telephone number, email address, Facebook account, and Twitter tag, place of employment, shoes, clothes, hair and makeup to begin to move toward what God has promised you.

We all understand that change can be uncomfortable, but if you are already uncomfortable, why not change? It just might be the shift you need to get in position to receive all that God has for you. Some of the foolishness and nonsense you allow in your life is like a well-conditioned lineman in football; it blocks you from receiving your blessings. Change your strategy, change your position!

> **Exodus 18:23**
>
> *"If thou shalt do this thing, and God command thee so, then thou shalt be able to endure, and all this people shall also go to their place in peace."*

THOUGHTS ON MY WAY OUT OF EGYPT:

MY EXODUS MOMENT

_____

_____

_____

_____

_____

_____

_____

_____

_____

_____

_____

THOUGHTS ON MY WAY OUT OF EGYPT:

MY EXODUS MOMENT

_____

_____

_____

_____

_____

_____

_____

_____

_____

_____

_____

CHAPTER 5

SHIFT

In the well-known Biblical story of the Exodus, we know that Pharaoh's army came after Moses and the Israelites. The Israelites were fearful and felt as though they were in a hopeless situation. The sea was to the east and the mountains were to the south and west. Then there was Pharaoh's army to the north. Moses and his people felt like they were trapped and it was impossible to escape. Have you found yourself in a situation or circumstance where you felt trapped with no way out? Did you act like the Israelites and blame someone else?

> "They said to Moses, "Why did you bring us to the desert to die? Weren't there any graves in Egypt? What have you done to us by bringing us out of Egypt? We told you in Egypt 'Leave us alone. Let us serve the Egyptians.' It would have been better for us to serve the Egyptians than to die here in the desert!"
> - Exodus 14:11-12.

Moses answered the people. He said, "Don't be afraid. Stand firm. You will see how the Lord will save you today. Do you see those Egyptians? You will never see them again. The Lord will fight for you. Just be still."

- Exodus 14:13-14

Have you ever considered that God may have intentionally led you to the place of being trapped so that he could expose His power to rescue you? Consider the following and how you see yourself in the same situation. God spoke to Moses and said, "Why are you crying out to me? Tell the people of Israel to move on. Hold your wooden staff out. Reach your hand out over the Red Sea to part the water. Then the people can go through the sea on dry ground" - Exodus 14:15-16. The Lord told Moses to stop praying and get moving!

How many times have you called the prayer line, Pastor, Intercessor, Ministry Leader, Grandma, Auntie or anyone else that you thought could "get a prayer through" and asked them to pray you out of something? A life style of prayer is critical, but as scripture has instructed us in James 2:17 "Thus also faith by itself, if it does not have works, is dead." We usually know what to do, but we allow fear to consume us. Instead we pray for more guidance as an excuse to delay taking action.

Simply put, sometimes it is just time "to get moving." It's time to shift—to shift our thinking, to shift our permission about the things we enable, permit and allow, to shift from our old ways of thinking and habits we've built.

The word "shift" is a verb and is defined as "to put (something) aside and replace it by another or others; change or exchange; to transfer from one place, position, person, etc., to another." How long should we allow the prison of our emotions to keep us in places that are nonproductive? Unhealthy relationships, abusive relationships, friendships that only benefit one person, unprogressive professional environments and complacent ministry relationships. When do we get courageous enough to just move on to something else?

Fear of the unfamiliar and unknown puts us in restraints and keeps us from progressing forward. We enable the familiar and comfortable to shackle us to things God never intended for us. We must take action to move from and past those people, places, and things that keep us in a perpetual state of unhappiness and stagnation to truly begin to realize God's real purpose in our lives.

Many of us live each day like we're driving a car with a bad transmission. We put the gear shift in drive, but we go nowhere. We put it in reverse planning to escape but we go nowhere. Then we just get out of the car feeling hopeless, worried about the cost of the repair and fail to realize that the cost of not repairing the transmission is greater than the cost of the repair. There is no price range associated with the mental, physical and emotional turmoil we place on ourselves and our bodies when we don't shift.

Yes, the next place will be different. There are a lot of unknowns and uncertainties but think back over your life and realize that the majority of your life has been an unknown. But you figured out how to navigate the road map of life even when you got distracted, detoured and outright lost.

Yes, you might lose a bit of time but ultimately you reach your destination. You might reach the destination on a flat tire, with a busted headlight or tail light, or even with some smoke coming from the exhaust. Nonetheless, you arrive in a new place.

We must subscribe to the old adage as quoted by Jean-Paul Sartre and Malcolm X "By any means necessary" will I get to the place God desires for me and I will shift to get there. Use all five gears! Even if you stay in first gear for a period of time, trust that your momentum will increase and you'll eventually excel in fifth gear.

Here are my three C's for helping you to shift:

(a) **Capacity** – defined as "the ability to receive or contain; actual or potential ability to perform, yield, or withstand." When we consider our capacity to change our circumstances, it should become evident that we are always in control of what we experience and what happens. A twelve-ounce cup has the capacity to hold twelve ounces of liquid. Why attempt to put sixteen ounces in something that was never designed to hold sixteen ounces? When you do that you make a complete mess, and then you have to spend time cleaning up the mess when all you had to do was use only the intended capacity. Many of us take on too many additional issues, concerns and problems that God never intended for us to take on. We have to release ourselves from the mindset that we can do it all. The scripture says "I can do all things through Christ who gives me strength" but it never said you had to do all things. God gives you wisdom, and He is even gracious enough to give you signs. We have to realize when it is time to say good bye to foolishness, nonsense and "Tom foolery" and wish them farewell. We must come to realize our own capacity and utilize that capacity to its fullest. We are not designed to take on the capacity of others along with ours. God wants to maximize our capacity and even confirmed that in Matthew 25:15 "To one he gave five talents, to another two, to another one--to each according to his individual capacity; and then started from home". (WEY). The only person we can change is ourselves. When Moses realized he had the capacity to part the Red Sea and deliver the people into the Promised Land, that is just what he did. It might take some longer than others to identify their capacity, but now is the time to start paying attention.

(b) **Commitment** – defined as "a pledge or promise; obligation; engagement; involvement." What are we truly willing to commit to when we decide to shift to another place? Shifting may cause you to experience loneliness, stress and lots of uncertainty. But are you truly willing to commit to the purpose God has for you and trust His word? Proverbs 16: 3(NKJV) "Commit your works to the Lord, and your thoughts will be established." Much like when you begin a new workout routine or exercise program. There is a period of time when you experience the "burn" and it can be intense and cause you to want to give up immediately. The Israelites spent 40 years in the wilderness. Are you really willing to spend the time, effort, energy, expense and exhaustion to get all that God has for you? That can mean that you experience some level of deprivation, denial and disruption to ultimately reach that place. But it does require that you uphold your promise and pledge to Him just like He committed His promises to you. We often want to "pimp" God and "test" Him on His word. Unlike the pimps on the street, He is not here today and gone tomorrow demanding "Better have my money." God is faithful, loyal and dedicated to seeing you fulfill your ordained destiny in Christ Jesus. But you must commit to Him in total submission so that He can truly begin a new work in you and bring it to completion as promised in Philippians 1:6 *"Being confident of this very thing, that he which hath begun a good work in you will perform it until the day of Jesus Christ."*

(c) **Consistency** - defined as "steadfast adherence to the same principles, course, form, etc.; agreement, harmony, or compatibility, especially correspondence or uniformity among the parts of a complex thing." According to 1 Timothy 3:7, "And he must have a good reputation with those outside the church, so that he will not fall into reproach and the snare of the devil." When you come to understand your capacity and identify your level of commitment, consistency will be required in everything you say and do. There is no compromise, no tethering and no moments of momentary lapses that cause you to fall back in the mindset, ways and behaviors that caused you to get to the place where you were bound and shackled. Yes, I am talking about those friendships that you have walked away from, relationships that you ended, and opportunities which really were a set of chains to prevent you from moving. You must recognize where you are going and that not everyone can have a voucher to ride along. Matthew 5:37 says, "But let your 'Yes' be 'Yes,' and your 'No,' 'No.' For whatever is more than these is from the evil one." This verse gives us the clear instruction of how we remain consistent and not cause others to be confused by our actions. If you have told your friends that you don't want to gossip, then being consistent means when the "tea is hot" you don't participate. Being consistent means when the phone pings after 10:00 p.m.; the text message reads "I need to talk to you…" and you've told that old flame that the fire is OUT! Go get your fire extinguisher and put it by your bed. Kindly respond that counseling is a "per hour" fee and you can schedule an appointment between 9 and 5. When you say you're going to do something, do it timely and in excellence so that God's glory is revealed every time. That's being consistent. Don't participate in any activities, conversations, actions, social media or anything that will discredit your character and bring dishonor to our heavenly Father. Call out the enemy, speak to the mountain. Decree and declare your godliness and holiness in all things at all times. Decide now to SHIFT!

John 14:26

"But the Comforter, which is the Holy Ghost, whom the Father will send in my name, he shall teach you all things, and bring all things to your remembrance, whatsoever I have said unto you."

THOUGHTS ON MY WAY OUT OF EGYPT:

MY SHIFT

_____

_____

_____

_____

_____

_____

_____

_____

_____

_____

_____

THOUGHTS ON MY WAY OUT OF EGYPT:

MY SHIFT

CHAPTER 6

A NEW DAY

Dawn

According to Lamentations 3:22-23, "It is of the Lord's mercies that we are not consumed, because his compassions fail not; they are new every morning: great is thy faithfulness." If we think about our lives and the trials and troubles we've endured, think about the life of Jesus Christ. His life story had a time of serving, exploring, teaching and testing. Like many of our life stories, we probably have memories or thoughts of how we journeyed down each of these paths. What we fully understand is that Jesus Christ endured a crucifixion and resurrection at the end of His story. "He endured one side to get to the other" (Joyce Meyer). Many of us must come to realize that we have experienced a crucifixion in our lives, and now is the time for the resurrection.

God has kept us and blessed us through many trials and tribulations. Now is the time to unpack the baggage of our past—and in some cases present—and move on. This is an exciting time because we can proclaim victory over the enemy and rejoice because we have won!

One of my favorite songs since I can remember developing an affinity for contemporary gospel music is "He's Preparing Me" as sung by Daryl Coley. The first verse of the song begins like this: "He's preparing me for something I cannot handle right now, He's making me ready, just because He cares, He's providing me with what I'll need, to carry out the next matter in my life." Every life experience is a period of preparation. Just like men and women who enlist in the military endure basic training, which at times is uncomfortable, we too have our time of training and preparation. And oh how uncomfortable it can be!

When you understand and trust the Word, you remember as promised in 2 Corinthians 5:17, "Therefore if any man be in Christ, he is a new creature: old things are passed away; behold all things are become new." I received a revelation when I researched the definition of the significance of a new day. I found the following on vocabulary.com: "Not just the beginning of a day, the noun dawn can refer to any beginning: as a verb, dawn can mean "become light" or "become clear!" This was so powerful and helped me to understand that when a "new day" comes, we begin to see things better; the darkness ceases and our lenses realign for clarity.

I thought about how each time I see my optometrist for my annual eye examination, during that process the doctor assesses for diseases, conditions, the anatomy of the eye, and my peripheral vision, all in an effort to determine the state of my vision.

Ultimately, there is a need to determine if anything has changed, if any adjustments are needed, and if a new prescription is required.

Now let's consider this spiritually. A prescription is technically an order written by a physician that indicates the required dosage and usage. When the Chief Physician writes you a new prescription, He is giving you instructions for the change in dosage required for your healing, deliverance, and restoration. It is glorious to know that God remains steadfast in His love for His children and adjusts as needed to keep us strong, virtuous, righteous and victorious.

We don't look in the rear view mirror to see where we are going, we look out the windshield which gives us an expanding range of perception as well as opportunities. The bumps in the road that you have encountered along the journey were just the push you needed to remind you that you are a living, breathing creature full of promise and potential. Even when your personal GPS did not calibrate properly and you ended up at a dead end or dangerous intersection, 1 Corinthians 10:13 reminds us that "There hath no temptation taken you but such as is common to man: but God is faithful, who will not suffer you to be tempted above that ye are able; but will with the temptation also make a way to escape, that ye may be able to bear it." You can never be too far off course to be beyond God's reach.

Destiny

Do you not know that you are a survivor? You have withstood the test, you overcame the hurdle, and you dodged every dart thrown your way. Yes, you were bruised, beaten, tattered and torn, but you were never broken or defeated in the spirit.

God's word so proficiently demonstrates Jesus' wilderness experience and illustrates how, with every temptation, Jesus fought mightily with His arsenal of weaponry and threw the Book at the enemy. In the midst of your wilderness experiences, you found yourself remembering and recalling the passages of scripture needed for you to throw a sucker punch back. God's word is our wilderness GPS (God's Positioning System), and it protects us from the lies that are designed and spoken to destroy us. When you permit Jesus to be your source of strength and peace, it allows Him to be your wilderness guide so that He would lead you from the wilderness of this world back to Eden again.

God wants us to listen to Him and follow Him completely. He frequently gives us reassurances of His presence. In the story from Exodus, God told Moses to lead the people toward the Red Sea. Now if you are like me, a non-swimmer, going towards the sea would seem like a ridiculous plan, but because Moses trusted God and understood the power of God through his relationship and conversation, Moses did not consider the request ridiculous like many of us would. This is the place where we must truly recognize the power and authority that God has given us to conquer the impossible.

Moses leads the people to the Red Sea and God demonstrates His power through Moses' staff and parts the seas for the people to safely cross into the Promise Land. Not only do they cross over safely, but He uses the same waters He parted to completely consume the approach of the enemy. What God is revealing to every overcomer who has been in bondage, endured oppression, depression, compression, recession, confession, aggression, regression and transgression, is that He is still able to do "exceedingly abundantly above all that we ask or think, according to the power that works in us" as stated in Ephesians 3:20. God has confirmed to you that you have the power to overcome and cross over every Red Sea in your life.

You have reached a pinnacle in your life. The time is now, your break through has come, the doors have opened and you have options. Reach in to your pockets, purses, satchels, back packs, cup holder, wristlet or whatever you are carrying and find your keys. Yes, your keys! The keys to unlock the chains of bondage, the keys to the Kingdom of greatness, the keys for you to reach and fulfill the destiny that God had always planned and purposed for you.

Every attack, every hindrance, every setback and setup, every failure, every bad, unhealthy, unfair and irresponsible relationship has been redeemed. You are now in a season of renewal, recognition, reward and fulfillment for every time you were overlooked, unappreciated, disrespected and criticized. God has turned it around for your good! He promised in His Word: "For I know the thoughts that I think toward you, saith the Lord, thoughts of peace, and not of evil, to give you an expected end" (Jeremiah 29:11). And as I have stated many times before, Proverbs 3:5-6 is clear, "Trust in the Lord with all thine heart; and lean not unto thine own understanding. In all thy ways acknowledge him, and he shall direct thy paths." You have won, victory is yours, and you can now declare, I AM Out of Egypt!

THOUGHTS ON MY WAY OUT OF EGYPT:

MY NEW DAY

_____

_____

_____

_____

_____

_____

_____

_____

_____

_____

_____

THOUGHTS ON MY WAY OUT OF EGYPT:

MY NEW DAY

CONCLUSION

As you can see, many of us live our lives like we are present day Israelites: fearful, intimidated, uncertain, not willing to take risk, not trusting others who may have been sent to deliver us into our Promise Land because they don't look, think or act like us. If we recognized that imploring some of the historical practices into our modern day, technologically advanced age, such as commitment, resilience, discipline and honor, we can overcome and defeat the attacks of the enemy every moment of every day.

Our beginning from childhood was designed to give us a point on the navigation map of life where to start. As we become more skilled at reading and navigating the map, we will recognize that the road to our destiny is full of rugged terrain that we must endure to reach our intended destinations. There will be roadblocks along the journey. Even during this experience, when I committed that I would write and publish my book, I have had to maneuver all types of road blocks, detour signs, dead ends and road work ahead to get here. I have endured two significant medical diagnoses, major surgeries, intense physical therapy and every other distraction that could come my way. Admittedly I got frustrated, angry and discouraged. I began to recognize that I had to come "Out of Egypt,"—my place of oppression and bondage about my past hurts, disappointments and abandonment to share my experience so that others would recognize that they too can come out.

I remembered the foundation on which my character was built by my parents and siblings in the beginning. The care, love, compassion, strength, resolve, commitment, discipline and faith that was repeatedly demonstrated in my presence that equipped me to be a conqueror and overcomer. There was no purpose or point in my remaining in a foreign land in the wilderness. I had to activate my authority to speak to every mountain in my life and activate my faith—even if it was only the size of a mustard seed—to propel me to my intended destiny.

I realized that I had the capacity to shift my focus, which in turn shifted my direction. When my direction changed, God gave me the endurance I needed to flee those people, places and practices that had attempted to abort my future—physically and emotionally abusive relationships, low self-esteem, lack of feeling worthy and capable, and financial lack. But GOD!

I can earnestly and honestly say that even as I continue to grow and mature, connecting the revelation of His Word and the power of praying without ceasing, even when the arrow points in one direction, as I keep my hands and heart lifted unto

CONCLUSION

God, He will deliver me out of the enemy's hand. Isaiah 54:17 states "No weapon that is formed against thee shall prosper; and every tongue that shall rise against thee in judgment thou shalt condemn. This is the heritage of the servants of the Lord, and their righteousness is of me, saith the Lord." I trust Him and acknowledge Him in all that I do.

When you come "Out of Egypt," you will no longer be concerned about being accepted by the world and the ways of the people, who likes or dislikes you, or who agrees or disagrees with you. When you come OUT, you know that you honor God through your lifestyle of worship and intercession. His acceptance and approval are His reward to you for your obedience, and no one else can give you that level of love, support and encouragement. I trust His promises and have the blessed assurance that He keeps me, protects me and loves me.

You might not fully come OUT of your oppression overnight. It might take weeks or even months or years. But KNOW and be confident that you will come OUT!

Just as with me, God wants to use you as an example; as a living epistle or testimony to others. He wants to let others see what He can do, IF we allow Him to go before us and lead us out of bondage. As you surrender all of your circumstances, roadblocks, shortcomings, and weaknesses to Him, He will show Himself faithful. As you slowly, but surely come out of your "Egypt" believe these words in the deepest places of your heart and spirit:

"Being confident of this very thing, that he which hath begun a good work in you will perform it until the day of Jesus Christ." (Philippians 1:6)

-Selah

Lamentations 3:22

"It is of the Lord's mercies that we are not consumed, because his compassions fail not."

THOUGHTS ON MY WAY OUT OF EGYPT:

MY NEW CONCLUSION

THOUGHTS ON MY WAY OUT OF EGYPT:

MY NEW CONCLUSION

_____

_____

_____

_____

_____

_____

_____

_____

_____

_____

THOUGHTS ON MY WAY OUT OF EGYPT:

MY NEW CONCLUSION

_____

_____

_____

_____

_____

_____

_____

_____

_____

_____

_____

THOUGHTS ON MY WAY OUT OF EGYPT:

MY NEW CONCLUSION

_____

_____

_____

_____

_____

_____

_____

_____

_____

_____

THOUGHTS ON MY WAY OUT OF EGYPT:

MY NEW CONCLUSION

THOUGHTS ON MY WAY OUT OF EGYPT:

MY NEW CONCLUSION

THOUGHTS ON MY WAY OUT OF EGYPT:

MY NEW CONCLUSION

_____

_____

_____

_____

_____

_____

_____

_____

_____

_____

THOUGHTS ON MY WAY OUT OF EGYPT:

MY NEW CONCLUSION

_____

_____

_____

_____

_____

_____

_____

_____

_____

_____

_____

ABOUT THE AUTHOR

Minister Tonya Renee McClure

Minster Tonya McClure, is a native of Atlanta, and grew up dancing, taking Ballet, Pointe, Tap and Jazz, Modern and African. She has studied at The Ailey School, where she was the recipient of a scholarship.

She has been an active member of Destiny World Church, in the metropolitan Atlanta area, since 2000 where she received her license as a minister of the Gospel in October 2010. Tonya served as the dance ministry leader and serves as a member of the ministerial alliance, mentoring program, and new members' ministry.

Tonya has completed Eagles International Training Institute (EITI) Dance 2006; Eagles International Leadership Institute (EILI) 2010 & 2014; Kingdom Ambassadors Ministerial Training (KAMT) 2011; Eagles International Intercessory Prayer Institute (EIIPI) 2012 & 2013. She was ordained to the office of Teacher in 2011 under International Covenant Life (ICL) Network. She is a member of the National Liturgical Dance Network (NLDN), International Dance Commission (IDC) and previously served as the Georgia state coordinator for Christian Dance Fellowship USA (CDFUSA).

Tonya enjoys teaching leadership development classes and equipping individuals to fulfill their God-ordained purpose. Tonya has served as the Georgia Co-Leader for Passion for Worship Dance Ministries International and teaches dance locally in the Atlanta area. Minister Tonya has been blessed to travel abroad to Malaysia, Bahamas, Barbados, Israel, Ghana West Africa, Scotland and Puerto Rico to study, teach and "advance the Kingdom." Tonya is a member of

Delta Sigma Theta Sorority, Inc. and has one son Ricky, daughter in-law Tiffany and grandson Reese Alexander.

For more information, please contact Tonya R. McClure at

770-739-1563

or visit

www.anointed2dance4him.org